OFFICE *Spa*

OFFICE *Spa*

Stress Relief for the Working Week

by Darrin Zeer

illustrations by Frank Montagna

CHRONICLE BOOKS

SAN FRANCISCO

Copyright © 2002 by **Darrin Zeer**.

Illustrations copyright © 2002 by **Frank Montagna**.
All rights reserved. No part of this book may be
reproduced in any form without written permission
from the publisher.

Library of Congress Cataloging-in-Publication Data available.

ISBN: 0-8118-3345-3

Manufactured in China.

Designed by **Vivien Sung**.

Distributed in Canada by Raincoast Books
9050 Shaughnessy Street
Vancouver, British Columbia V6P 6E5

10 9 8 7 6 5 4 3

Chronicle Books LLC
85 Second Street
San Francisco, California 94105

www.chroniclebooks.com

It isn't where you are ...

It's how you are.

Contents

QUick *HELP guide*

INTROduction

Life has never been more fast-paced and stressful than it is in the twenty-first century. Most of us have become expert multitaskers. Cell phones, e-mail, and pagers have made it possible to be on call twenty-four hours a day, and the pressure and strain of juggling day-to-day tasks can leave you feeling mentally drained and physically worn out.

It's no mystery that when you're rested and healthy, your work is more satisfying, you make fewer mistakes, and you derive more enjoyment from the workplace. Of course you want to be healthy and happy, and your company wants you to be healthy and happy, but the challenge is how?

The spa is a centuries-old practice that is the perfect antidote for today's crazed workweek. Spas rejuvenate the mind, body, and spirit with exercises such as yoga and meditation, and luxurious baths, massages, and exotic wraps, as well as nourishing foods. But where can you find a spa when you need it most? And who can afford time away from the office to indulge?

Office Spa offers more than fifty simple, stress-relieving exercises that you can enjoy right at your desk. None of them takes much time. Start your day with a quick wake-up meditation. Treat yourself to a stimulating herbal-tea steam while you return calls. Nurture yourself during those few free moments in between projects and meetings. Turn your cubicle into an oasis of calm. Try some relaxing reflexology during your lunch break, and after a hard day let your cares float away in a soothing bath.

Each day of the week has a different theme. Feeling tense on a Tuesday? Worn out on a Wednesday? Need to focus on a Friday? Turn to the section for that day of the week for tips on refreshing and rejuvenating yourself. If you have specific needs, look to the Quick Help Guide on page 9.

Work can be chaotic and stressful. Why not make each day an *Office Spa* day? You'll be glad you did.

the FIVE *golden RULES* of the OFFICE *spa*

I   I will breathe deeply and slowly,
relaxing my body.

2   I will keep things simple,
moving forward one step at a time.

3   I will focus on each step calmly.

4   I will not stress out about
the little things.

5   I will treat myself to an *Office Spa*
break whenever the need arises.

MELLow

Monday

Dip your toes in *before you dive* . . .

PRE-work *PAMPERING*
morning MASK

This simple mask is a wonderful skin softener and is excellent for dry, sensitive skin. Breakfast will never be the same.

Ingredients
2 tablespoons plain yogurt

2 tablespoons uncooked oatmeal

A few drops of honey

Directions
1 In a bowl, mix together the yogurt and oatmeal.

2 Add the honey and stir until smooth.

3 Gently massage the mixture onto your face, moving your fingertips in a circular motion and avoiding the eye area.

4 Leave mask on for five minutes while you prepare your breakfast or take a peek at the morning paper.

5 Rinse off the mask with warm water and feel your face pleasantly tingling.

monday *MORNING blues*

Need a quick pick-me-up? Stimulate your senses with
aromatherapy. The oldest form of medicine known to human-
kind, aromatherapy promotes health and well-being through
the use of essential oils, the most concentrated essence of
a plant. Ylang-ylang essential oil has a soft fragrance that
helps calm anxiety. You can purchase a small vial at a health-
food store or beauty shop. Store it in a desk drawer, and
when you arrive at work on Monday morning, open the
bottle and take a whiff.

Remember, it's Monday—take it easy today.

HERbal *TEA* ceremony

Are you ready to go beyond the tea bag? Create a "tea corner" on your desk with a nice Japanese or English teapot, some teacups, honey, and a selection of teas.

When you are ready for a break with a co-worker or client, share some tea. Get out a tea ball or strainer to hold the herbs. Add 2 tablespoons of herbs for each cup and place inside the teapot. Pour hot water into the pot, cover, and let steep for a few minutes.

Pour the tea into the cups and sweeten if desired. Peace can come from simple activities.

say "CHI"

In many parts of Asia it is believed that good health is maintained by a flow of energy called *chi*. By pressing particular points on the face you can stimulate *chi*, relieve tension, and bring a glow to your cheeks. Let your fingers do the walking.

1 With the pointer finger of each hand, find a spot on each side of your face and press gently but firmly for a few moments. Do not rub or scrub. Continue by pressing different spots around your face.

2 With your fingertips, rhythmically tap all over your face like raindrops.

3 To stimulate circulation, gently pound your cheeks and forehead with loose fists.

4 End the treatment by gently placing your hands over your face to soothe.

inner *ORDER*

Your workweek will go much more smoothly if you take some time on Monday morning to write your anxieties away. Appointments, to-do lists, deadlines—get these out of your head and onto paper and you'll feel the stress fade away. Check items off throughout the week and see how much you accomplish.

skin-*so*-SMOOTHIE

Celebrate Bring-Your-Blender-to-Work Day! If you have a freezer at work, stock it with bags of frozen fruit, such as strawberries, blueberries, blackberries, and mangoes. If you don't have a freezer in the office, stop by the grocery store and pick up some fresh items.

> 1 peeled banana, broken up
>
> 1 cup assorted fruit
>
> 1/2 cup milk, soy milk, or nonfat yogurt
>
> Handful of ice cubes (not necessary if using frozen fruit)
>
> Protein powder (optional)

Put all ingredients into the blender and blend until smooth.

ADD *some* YIN AND *YANG*
to your *CUP*!

Just for the fun of it, make a yin-and-yang smoothie! Make
two shakes using a different fruit for each, for example,
strawberry and pineapple. First blend the strawberries and
fill two clear glasses halfway with the pink mixture. Then
blend the pineapple and slowly top off the cups with the
yellow mixture. Stand back and appreciate the colors. It's
good-looking and good for you! Perfect for sharing with
your cube mate.

STAY on the BALL

Work out while you're working! Swiss balls are large, inflated rubber balls that are available at any back-care store. Sitting atop the ball helps your posture by forcing you to constantly shift to maintain your balance. For maximum benefits, use the Swiss ball for your desk chair.

Feeling frustrated? Bounce!

1 Sit comfortably on the ball with your back straight. Imagine a string is attached to the top of your head, pulling your head straight up toward the ceiling.

2 Bend your knees and spread your feet wide until you find your balance.

3 Bounce slowly and breathe.

You'll be surprised at the workout you can get!

 Confine yourself to the present.
—Marcus Aurelius

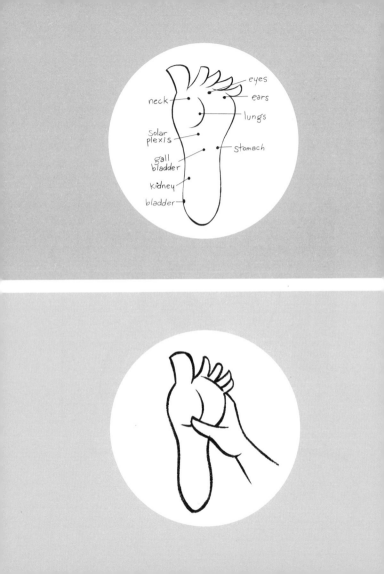

relaxing REFLEXology

Reflexology is the art of applying pressure to specific points on the feet to assist circulation and ease aches and pains in the body. The quick reflexology routine given below is easy to do anytime. Since there are thousands of nerve endings on the feet, it's hard to "miss the point."

1 Remove your shoes.

2 Cross one leg over the other, resting your ankle comfortably just above your knee.

3 Relax as you begin to knead your foot, using the strength of your thumbs to apply pressure to the spots given in the diagram.

4 Take it easy; don't hurt yourself. To apply more pressure, use your knuckles.

5 When you find a sensitive spot, hold the pressure and take deep, gentle breaths.

6 Work in a circular motion over your entire foot.

7 To finish, knead in larger circles, moving above your ankles to your calves.

POST-work *PAMPERING*
cleopatra's MILK BATH

Whew! You made it through another Monday. Treat yourself to an extra-special bath. The lactic acid in milk softens, soothes, and creates velvety-smooth skin. It is a known fact that Cleopatra loved to luxuriate in a warm milk bath.

1 Run warm water into a bathtub.

2 Add a quart of milk to the running water (a pound of powdered milk works also).

3 Create atmosphere by dimming the lights and lighting candles in safe positions around the tub. Put on some soothing music.

4 Have bottled water, towels, and a bath pillow close at hand.

5 Sprinkle rose petals in the water for extra pampering.

6 Sink in and relax.

*Learn to be silent. Let your quiet mind
listen and absorb.* —Pythagoras

TRanQUIL
Tuesday

Ready or not, *here I come!*

PRE-work *PAMPERING*
GREAT HAIR day

For clear thoughts and extra-soft hair with a sweet apple scent, this massage stimulates the scalp and alleviates tension headaches.

1. Combine 2 cups distilled water with 2 tablespoons of apple cider.

2. In the shower, pour the mixture onto shampooed and conditioned hair.

3. Leave on for 3–5 minutes while you close your eyes, relax your body, and slowly massage your scalp, working your fingertips in circular motions all around your head.

4. Rinse your hair thoroughly when finished.

Kindness in words creates confidence.
   Kindness in thinking creates profoundness.
Kindness in giving creates love. —Lao Tzu

HEALTHful honey

Besides its golden sweetness, honey is a food unsurpassed in energy value. With valuable trace vitamins and minerals, it's a healthful sweetener and a great alternative to cane sugar. Keep a squeezable container at your desk to add to both hot and cold beverages. Or for a sweet and healthy snack, spread it on some whole-wheat toast or a bran muffin.

Meeting *MIST*

Let lavender set the mood! The scent of lavender alleviates stress-related symptoms such as headaches, insomnia, anxiety, and fatigue.

1 Fill a clean spray bottle with 6–8 tablespoons of cool water.

2 Add 2–4 drops of lavender essential oil and shake.

3 With your eyes closed, mist your face.

4 Take a nice deep breath.

5 Organize your thoughts and spend a moment focusing on your agenda.

6 Keep the bottle tightly closed and treat yourself and your desk area to a spritz throughout the day.

Tension is who you think you should be.
Relaxation is who you are. —Chinese Proverb

KEYboard *recovery*

To avoid computer strain and keep your hands in mint condition, take a break after every 15 minutes of typing. Make the most of your breaks by giving yourself a helping hand. Keep your favorite moisturizer at your desk and give yourself a soothing hand massage. Working certain pressure points can help relieve work stress.

1 Spread moisturizer thickly onto your hands.

2 Interlace your fingers and using your thumb, massage the palm of your other hand.

3 For deeper treatment, search out sore spots, press with the thumb, and hold for 10 seconds.

4 Once you've found all the sore spots, switch hands.

5 Remember to breathe deeply into your belly and relax your shoulders while massaging.

6 To complete, interlace your fingers and squeeze and massage both hands at once.

7 Notice the fast tension relief!

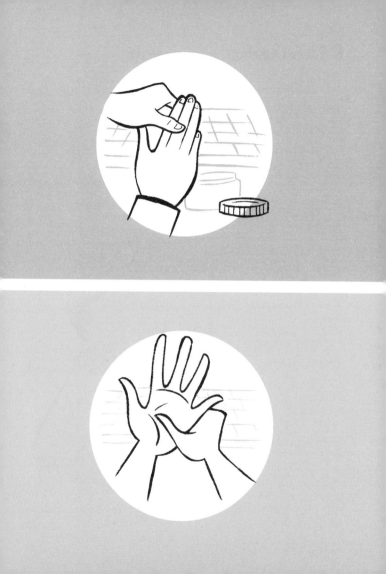

IMAGine for a *moment* . . .

Take a deep breath and imagine for a moment hiking through the snow-capped mountains.

Savor the scent and feel the magic of nature.

Let time stand still!

ICED ginger-*lemon*-honey
PICK-*ME*-UP *tea*

Ginger has great rejuvenating properties, and lemon is very soothing for cold symptoms. Add honey and you have a sweet and healthy beverage. Next time you're feeling run-down, brew a pot of this invigorating tea.

Ingredients

2 ginger tea bags

2 tablespoons lemon juice (about half a fresh lemon)

2 tablespoons honey

2 cups hot water

lemon wedges

Directions

1 Place the 2 ginger tea bags in a bowl. Add the lemon juice and honey.

2 Pour hot water over the ingredients and let steep for 10 minutes. Let tea cool until luke warm.

3 Pour the tea into 2 large glasses full of ice.

4 Garnish with lemon wedges and share with a workmate.

INSTANT *inspiration*

Need a refreshing inspiration for your next project? Eucalyptus essential oil will help clear your thoughts. Dab a few drops on a piece of paper and breathe in the aroma. If you feel congested or sense a cold coming on, put 4 drops of eucalyptus in a cup of hot water. (For increased effectiveness, place a towel over your head and breathe in the steam.) The strong scent will revive you.

 Worry often gives a small thing a big shadow.

—Swedish Proverb

Take a WALK on the *WILD SIDE*

Getting too intimate with your desk? Becoming codependent with your computer? Time to make a run for it! For a heavy dose of nature, take yourself to the local park. Just a few minutes in a green space will put things into perspective.

Samurai *POSTURE*

Easy Ergonomics!

The Samurai is renowned for the ability to move gracefully —calm and focused, each movement in harmony with the next. Practice moving in your workspace with the precision of a Samurai warrior.

1 Face your work head-on! Keep realigning your posture toward your next project.

2 Don't hold your body rigid.

3 Find your balance and remain calm and focused.

4 Use your entire body with each task—whether you're lifting a piece of paper or a large box, make sure each part of your body is aligned.

5 Avoid unnecessary physical strain.

6 Scan yourself from head to toe and take deep, gentle breaths to release tension.

 I came, I saw, I conquered. —Julius Caesar

If the SHOE *FITS*, wear *it!*

In an average day, a person will take more than 7,000 steps. In an average lifetime, a person will walk more than 100,000 miles. The message: Be good to your feet and they'll serve you well for miles to come. Here are a couple of tips:

1 Keep a pair of running shoes at your desk for unexpected errands. If your shoes are comfortable, you'll be inspired to walk farther.

2 For those of you burning the midnight oil, keep a pair of cozy slippers at your desk. When the office starts to quiet down, take off your shoes and put on your fuzzy slippers. Your feet will thank you.

POST-meeting *POWER NAP*

Research shows that when your energy wanes and your
creativity is stifled, an afternoon nap can be just the cure.
Some companies even have nap rooms with lounge chairs
and peaceful music. Others have a comfortable couch or
chair in the lunchroom. Seek out a quiet nook, maybe even
a bench outside in the sun. Set your watch alarm and let
yourself drift off. Even five minutes can make a difference.

FEELING *E-motional?*

Surf and ye shall find. Ask yourself: What is bothering me today? Deadlines? Backache? Summarize your frustration in one word or phrase. Type your word or phrase into your favorite Internet search engine. Check out some of the responses. Are they helpful? Sometimes looking at things from a different angle can provide unexpected insight.

Forget-ABOUT-*your*-TROUBLES
BATH FORMULAS

These essential oil combinations can be combined with Epsom salts.

* Relaxation Formula: 4 drops each of lavender and ylang-ylang
* Invigorating Formula: 4 drops each of eucalyptus and peppermint

Enjoy a cup of herbal tea before your bath; it will encourage perspiration and leave you even more refreshed.

WiSE

Wednesday

Full speed ahead, *without the dread!*

PRE-work *PAMPERING*

Bask in the warmth of a sunrise. Wake up a little early today. Go for a walk, or just sit outside. Notice how peaceful the world is at rest.

Somehow Mother Nature knows how to reignite the flame within. Keep this inspired, relaxed zest for life during the busy times of the day.

LOG-on *STEAM*

Relax your tired face and stimulate your senses. Peppermint is a great natural decongestant and also invigorates the mind.

1 Brew a hot cup of peppermint herbal tea.

2 Slowly lower your face over the cup.

3 Close your eyes for a moment.

4 Inhale deeply.

5 Enjoy the pleasant scent.

6 Feel the heat penetrating the pores of your skin.

7 Relax into the experience.

get *GROUNDED*

Does your to-do list have you running in circles? Next time you're at the beach or in the park, find a smooth, pocket-sized rock that feels comfortable in the palm of your hand. Keep it in your pocket or within easy reach on your desk. When you can't get off the treadmill of life, take out your stone and squeeze it. Notice your focus return and calm settle over you.

IMAGine for a *MOMENT* . . .

Walking on a deserted beach.

The clear blue ocean on a sunny day.

A gentle, cool breeze blowing.

Let your thoughts wander.

SEAweed *RAP*

Carrying a workload that's just too much? Grab a workmate and share your feelings over sushi. Be sure to listen as well as talk. Notice how refreshed you feel once you lighten your load. This simple practice has profound results. Try it with a new person each week. This is a great way to make new friends.

A *FRESH* approach

Is it your turn to be in the spotlight? If you have a presentation to give or a meeting to participate in, here are some refreshing tools to assist your delivery and calm your nerves. Keep the kit handy.

- ✳ Mint toothpaste and travel toothbrush for a confident smile.
- ✳ Peppermint mouthwash.
- ✳ Mint tea to soothe the nerves and tummy.

SPA *mix*

Want more than the vending machine offers? Create your own personalized trail mix and keep it in a bag or container in the office refrigerator. Here are some ideas:

- ✳ Raw unsalted almonds
- ✳ Raw unsalted walnuts
- ✳ Unsulfured raisins
- ✳ Lightly salted sunflower seeds
- ✳ Raw pumpkin seeds
- ✳ Dried unsulfured apricots
- ✳ Carob or chocolate chips
- ✳ A shake of cinnamon and nutmeg

Fill a few plastic bags with trail mix and pass them out to other weary workers.

 Sorrow shared is halved and joy shared is doubled.

—North American Indian Saying

Acu*PRESSURE* in the **AFTER**noon

Taking your shoes off when walking around the office
or when sitting at your desk can be very rejuvenating and
helpful for sore feet. For extra relief for backaches and
headaches, try this easy under-the-desk technique.

1 Place a golf ball or rolling pin on the floor under your
   feet.

2 While sitting, roll the sole of each foot firmly over the
   ball or rolling pin.

WALK *your* *WORRIES* away

Something troubling you? A deadline? Too many to-do's?
A co-worker? Refresh yourself and get some exercise, too,
by taking a brisk walk. Put on your walking shoes and try
climbing some stairs. Bring your knees up high for an extra
challenge. Walk it off. Or, for a gentler workout, take a tour
around the office. Walk slowly and step out of your troubles
by focusing on each step. Feel the entire sole of each foot as
it touches the ground. By the end of your walk, your troubles
will have gone. Move on to the next task with enthusiasm!

POST-work *PAMPERING*
incredible cukes!

You just got home and you're worn out, but your day planner has you down for a business dinner. Cucumber is the key to rejuvenating tired skin. This combination foot and eye treatment is a great way to refresh yourself before heading out the door again.

1. Fill a basin large enough for your feet with cool water.

2. Cut 3 cucumbers into medium slices.

3. Keep 2 slices for your eyes and throw the rest into the basin.

4. Lie back in a comfortable chair.

5. Place the basin on a towel by your feet, and keep another towel handy.

6. Place your feet in the basin, tilt your head back, and place a cucumber slice over each closed eye.

7. Relax and enjoy the nourishing break while listening to some soothing music.

You will feel completely refreshed as you head back out.

Life is not so short but that there is always time for courtesy. —Ralph Waldo Emerson

Thought*FUL*
Thursday

You are almost there—*enjoy the climb!*

PRE-work *PAMPERING*

Morning Wake-up Meditation

Before you get out of bed, spend ten minutes
becoming present.

1 Sit up and relax your body.

2 Take deep, gentle breaths.

3 Calm yourself.

4 Focus on your day.

5 Prepare to take action.

Question: What area of your life needs organizing?

CAR Com*fort*

Why not turn your vehicle into a sanctuary? Make an altar by placing a flower or your favorite picture on your dashboard. Create scents and sounds that are personal and peaceful. Challenge yourself to remain calm and enjoy the moment as you move through rush-hour traffic. Driving is a meditation on staying sharp and alert to your surroundings. Keep a small carry bag handy with a nice change of clothes and a toiletry kit in it. Relaxation is being prepared for the unexpected. Your car is also a great place to escape to during the day when you need peace, quiet, and privacy.

SHIATSU tension **TAMER**

Shiatsu is a Japanese finger pressure massage. It encourages the flow of energy in the body. This self-treatment is very energizing and stress relieving. It doesn't require massage oil and can easily be performed over clothing. Try it on your arms, legs, or wherever you feel a muscle ache.

1 Get comfortable in your seat.

2 Begin to relax your body, muscle by muscle.

3 Press your thumb or fingertips into any area where muscles are tight.

4 Apply firm pressure for five seconds, then move to another spot.

5 Take a deep breath and focus on relaxing your body as you apply the pressure.

Don't be surprised if you feel the benefits immediately!

ZEN and the *ART of organizaTION*

A clean desk makes for a clear mind. Create order in a calm, meditative way.

1 Pay attention to the busyness of your mind.

2 What judgments or frustrations do you carry?

3 Breathe in rhythm to your movements.

4 Enjoy the challenge of bringing your space into perfect order. Every item has its proper place.

When finished, your mind will feel open and light.

HA*RA* power

When it comes to massage, the abdominal area rarely gets any attention. Stomach massage can provide relief for indigestion, tension, and menstrual cramps. In Japan the entire stomach area is referred to as the *hara*, and it is considered to be the energy center for the entire body. To massage yourself:

1. Place the palm of your hand near your navel.

2. Make gentle circles around your navel in a clockwise motion.

3. Try pressing with your fingertips as you continue to slowly circle.

4. If you find a sore spot, stop and hold the pressure for a moment, and breathe deeply into your belly.

5. At the end of the session hold your hand still over your navel for a few moments.

6. Take deep breaths, and let your shoulders relax.

MISO *SOUP* for the *SOUL*

For hundreds of years the Japanese have enjoyed nourishing protein-rich miso soup. Made from soybeans, miso is a great source of compounds that help the body defend itself against illness. There are now excellent instant miso soup mixes at most health-food stores. Keep some at your desk for a quick hot meal anytime. Sip it surreptitiously in that afternoon meeting. No one will know you're eating your lunch.

EX*OTIC* mind MOTIVATOR

Mix up a batch of this powerful aromatic massage lotion and keep some at your desk.

1 Dilute 6 drops of sandalwood essential oil with 4 teaspoons sunflower, almond, or olive oil.

2 Rub a few drops onto your hands and arms.

3 Breathe in the powerful scent for instant inspiration.

 Patience is the best remedy for every trouble.
—Titus Maccius Platus

BURNING the *MIDNIGHT* OIL
spa kit

Keep these supplies handy for those unavoidable late nights.

* Fuzzy slippers
* Candles
* Sparkling water
* To-go menus from your favorite restaurants
* Energy bars
* Getting sleepy? Do a sound check in the office and turn up the tunes!

Remember when you were at your best?
Now be there again! —Author unknown

ELEVate *your MIND*

The elevator is one area with no distractions. Take a ride for some time out.

1 Position yourself at the rear of the elevator.

2 Stand comfortably with your knees slightly bent.

3 Watch the numbers rise or fall in unison with your breath.

4 When your floor arrives you will be calm and centered.

You can't do it right, you can't get it wrong.
You can only let go. —The Lady

GET un*plugged!*

Sometimes you just need to unhook.

1 Disconnect all your communication devices and just sit.

2 Set a time limit and hold to it.

3 Focus on the sounds of the office but don't get hooked into business.

4 Scan your body from head to toe, relaxing each area one at a time.

5 Take a deep, gentle breath to help calm yourself.

Post-WORK *PAMPERING*
urban REVIVAL

Here's a great bath to replenish your skin. Chinese doctors have prescribed white-wine baths for many years. Wine balances and detoxifies the skin, combating the effects of pollution as well as soothing sunburns. Pour one glass for you, and the rest into the tub. Drinks on you!

1. Run a bath.

2. Add half a bottle of white wine (and fill a glass for yourself).

3. Add a few drops of lavender or chamomile essential oil to the water for a relaxing aroma.

4. Have some drinking water close at hand and enjoy the medicinal soak.

Fulfill*ING*
Friday

Deliver the goods and *wrap it up.*

PRE-work *PAMPERING*
COLD plunge . . .

Because Friday is a day of celebration, start things off with a splash. Many elite spas feature a cold plunge. Rinsing off with very cold water refreshes the skin and closes your pores.

Begin with a warm shower and slowly change the temperature to cold. When the water gets cold your natural tendency will be to tighten up. Instead, focus for a few moments on breathing deeply and calmly, relaxing your body. It's hard to believe, but you can get comfortable in a cold shower. Egads! You may enjoy it so much, you'll want to start every day with a cold plunge.

He who fears he will suffer, already suffers because of his fear. —Michael de Montaigne

FLOwer POWER

Add a little nature to your workspace by turning your office into a Japanese garden. For those with green thumbs, orchids and Japanese bonsai are good selections. For the gardening impaired, a Christmas cactus or a palm is appropriate for its hardiness. It's also nice to place flowers on your desktop that will add color and a pleasant scent. Simply hold the flowers under your nose and breathe in for inspiration.

CHAMOMILE *compress*

Still suffering from computer eyestrain? Chamomile reduces swelling and is a very relaxing herbal drink.

1 Brew a cup of hot chamomile tea using two tea bags.

2 Remove the tea bags from the cup and set aside to cool on a plate.

3 When the tea bags are still warm but cool enough to touch, lean back, close your eyes, and gently place one bag onto each eyelid.

4 Rest for a few minutes with your eyes closed.

5 When the eye compresses have cooled, remove them and enjoy your tea.

All comes at the proper time to him who knows how to wait. —Saint Vincent de Paul

BRIEFcase *FENG* SHUI

A place for everything, and everything in its place. Feng shui is the art of placement. When your things are in order, you can relax, knowing that you are prepared and organized. Start with your briefcase or handbag. Spend time on the details: stock pens, pencils, erasers, an extra cell battery, envelopes, stamps. Clean out old receipts and scraps of paper. The stress relief you will derive from being organized is worth it. Next Monday, you will reap the benefits of time spent today in preparation.

 There is no happiness where there is no wisdom.

—Sophocles

GINSENG *zing*

Is your aching body keeping you pinned to your seat? For centuries ginseng has been recognized for its energizing properties. It provides a great boost when you need to bench-press your tired body out of your chair.

1 Prepare a hot cup of ginseng tea (available at most stores).

2 Try putting in a few drops of pure ginseng extract for an extra kick.

3 Add some honey or maple syrup.

4 Take a deep breath, and wait for the power surge.

EYE *energizer*

Tired eyes are a common side effect of computer use. Often, people forget to blink when staring at a computer screen.

To alleviate eyestrain and stress:

1 Refocus every ten minutes by looking out the window or around the office.

2 Roll your eyes in a circles, making sure to roll in both directions.

3 Once an hour close your eyes and let your face relax.

For soothing relief:

1 Rub your palms together quickly to warm them.

2 Place your palms gently over your closed eyes.

3 Hold them over your eyes until the heat dissipates.

4 Take a relaxing breath.

KA*RATE* CHOP your CUBE *mate*

Through thick and thin, your office mates stand by your side. It's payback time!

1. Ask a workmate permission to massage him and stand behind him as he sits in his chair.

2. Do a series of gentle, short, rapid karate chops on his shoulders.

3. Work into the sore muscles along the spine.

4. Avoid bones, only do muscle!

5. Inquire about the pressure and adjust to his request.

6. Have him lean forward so you can reach the upper back on both sides of his spine.

7. Tell the recipient to close his eyes and take a breath, relaxing his shoulders.

Your workmates will be grateful for their revived muscles and refreshed minds.

Be kind, for everyone you meet is fighting a hard battle. —Plato

POST-work *PAMPERING*
BED *retreat*

The skin is the largest organ of the body. If you are sleep-deprived, your skin will show it. Make sure you get seven to nine hours of sleep, and you will go into the weekend rosy-cheeked and refreshed.

1 Rent some relaxing videos.

2 Light a few candles, dim the lights, and turn your phone ringer off.

3 Don't forget to turn off your alarm!

4 Prepare some calming chamomile or peppermint tea before bedtime.

5 Dab a drop of lavender on a tissue and place it on your pillow for a soothing scent.

MANICURE and PEDICURE
while you SLEEP

When you're ready for bed, prepare this miniwrap for your hands and feet. Apply a generous amount of rich, natural moisturizer to your hands and feet. Pull a pair of cotton gloves or socks over your hands and put a pair of cotton socks on your feet. When you awake, your hands and feet will be remarkably softer.

STRESS *survival* KITS

Here are some *Office Spa* kits that will help soothe and relax you all day long.

Aromatherapy Travel Kit

Create a handy aromatherapy kit for home, office, and on-the-go. You'll need a small pouch that fits the five essential oil vials:

* Eucalyptus—cool and energizing decongestant
* Ylang-ylang—uplifting and balancing, soothes mental fatigue
* Lavender—relaxing, relieves tension and aids sleep
* Peppermint—stimulating and reviving, aids digestion
* Sandalwood—warm and exotic, calming

Home Stress Survival Kit

It's nice to have supplies at home for pre- and post-work relaxation. Pamper yourself through the weekend. Don't let the spa end on Friday.

* Aromatherapy Travel Kit (above)
* Epsom salts, candles, incense
* Pumice stone and loofah scrub brushes
* Natural moisturizing cream

Desk Stress Survival Kit

Keep this kit handy for refreshment and rejuvenation. You'll need:

* A teapot and some teacups
* A selection of teas—peppermint, chamomile, ginger, ginseng, and green tea
* Sparkling water and fresh fruit
* Miso soup and other natural-soup packets
* Trail mix and power bars
* 2 small plastic bottles, one for aromatherapy spray and the other for massage oil
* A golf ball or rolling pin for feet
* Your favorite plants and flowers

BioGRAPHIES

cole kaplan

Darrin Zeer is also the author of *Office Yoga*. He has spa experience with the Four Seasons Resort, Glen Ivy Hot Springs, and the Golden Door Spa. He spent seven years in Asia traveling and studying the Eastern arts of healing.

Darrin currently lives in California and Hawaii. He spends his time writing and consulting for individuals and companies, helping them to be more calm, balanced, and effective in their work and personal lives. He is also involved in the Miracle of Love Intensive. This six-day San Francisco–based intensive attracts some eighty participants each month from around the world.

If you or your company would like to contact the author, you can visit his Web site at **www.relaxyoga.com.**

Frank Montagna is a Los Angeles–based freelance illustrator whose work has appeared in a variety of publications including *New York* magazine, the *Wall Street Journal, Cosmo Girl, Modern Bride,* and *Glamour Germany.* He also works in television as a production and character designer, and has done animation work for Walt Disney Feature Animation and MTV. This is his first book.

ACK**NOW**ledg**ments**

Special thanks to my editor Mikyla Bruder, assistant editor Jodi Davis, and designer Vivien Sung. I also want to thank my nieces and nephews: Dustin, Stephanie, Mitchel, Ryan, Brayden, Conor, Lucas, Corbin, Isaac, Paul, and Carlund, for their courage and honesty.

 Every single soul is the most precious gem.

—Kalindi La Gourasana ♪